SOCIAL DANCE

FOR STUDENTS AND TEACHERS

By

I. F. WAGLOW, M. Ed.

Assistant Professor of Physical Education

University of Florida

WM. C. BROWN COMPANY
Publishers
DUBUQUE, IOWA

Manufactured by WM. C. BROWN CO. INC., Dubuque, Iowa
Printed in U. S. A.

Foreword

There is no more popular recreational activity than social dancing. A casual glance at the participants (and the observers) on any dance floor, however, is adequate evidence of the need for good teaching. Modern schools are beginning to meet this challenge by providing instruction for boys and girls from the junior high through the senior high school years; classes in social dance are eagerly sought by great numbers of students in colleges and universities, by teenagers and adults in community recreation programs. Ability in this activity is a distinct social advantage; it provides youth with an important and widely used carry-over skill, and is a popular, enjoyable asset at all age levels.

Teaching and learning are best when creatively approached and dance lends itself particularly well to this method. For this reason, Mr. Waglow deliberately has avoided set lesson plans. The basic materials are here; many useful teaching suggestions and progressions are included. The final organization of the material, however, its use and presentation becomes an individual matter, depending upon the teacher, the needs and interests and abilities of the particular class, or the special learner. Mr. Waglow has made a real contribution by writing on this subject in a very practical and understandable manner. His book should prove valuable both to students and teachers; it contains adaptable and appropriate material for beginners and the more experienced. It is a pleasant thought to believe that as a result of Mr. Waglow's efforts more boys and girls and adults will approach the dance floor with confidence, with skill, and with the attitude of creative fun.

Aileene Lockhart
Associate Professor of Education and
Physical Education
University of Southern California
Los Angeles

Preface

The purpose of this book is to provide a guide for class or self instruction in social dancing. It is hoped that it will assist the teacher and the student toward a better and fuller understanding of social dance. It includes the minimum essentials of each of the rhythms, as well as a graded progression to a higher level of competency. It is hoped that a level of skill will be reached to provide continued participation in the dance by all age groups.

In many school situations there has been the inclusion of square, tap, and modern dance. In recent years there has been a growing increase in the number of schools that have placed social dancing in the curriculum of the school program.

Many of the books written about social dancing have been done by professional dancers with the result that the educational aspect of dancing has not been touched upon. It is the hope of the author that this book will assist the teacher in presenting social dancing to large groups as well as individuals.

It will also provide a ready reference for the student in all areas concerned with social dancing.

Although the book is broken down into various chapters, it is hoped that the presentation of the materials will be in such a style that a complete integration of the various phases of social dancing will take place.

In the presentation of the step patterns, the gentleman's part is given in detail and it is assumed that the lady's part would be in reverse. However, where the lady's part is not in reverse, her part is given in the same detailed manner as the gentleman's part.

The author is indebted to his colleagues who encouraged him and provided him with the opportunity to teach social dancing in an educational situation, as well as to the many students who taught and inspired him in the area of social dancing.

I. F. Waglow

Gainesville, Florida
September, 1953

Contents

CHAPTER I
Introduction

Social dancing has contributed a great deal to the recreation, amusement, and enrichment of lives in our present day society. It has given many benefits to various age groups. Some of the specific benefits that an individual receives from social dance are as follows:

1. Social dancing gives an opportunity for social contacts.

2. Dancing breaks down reserves and provides group activities with opportunities for individual participation.

3. It helps to develop grace and poise.

4. The social contacts made in dancing provide an opportunity to cultivate good manners.

5. Social dancing furnishes an opportunity for recreation.

6. It has a health value physically and psychologically.

7. It gives the individual an opportunity to express himself rhythmically.

8. Since dance is an expression of an individual, it has art value.

There are many individuals who have not had the opportunity to engage in this type of activity. However, there is reason why the educational system should provide this type of experience for its students. Since the school is concerned with all around development of the individual, social dancing has a definite contribution to make to this development.

Knowledge of skills and the teaching processes, along with the desire to teach others, serves as an ideal foundation for the teacher of social dance in the school situation.

The use of the term "social dance" has different connotations for various individuals. Many times to the elementary school student it is something to be avoided, to the high school student it is an activity engaged in by a certain few, and to the college student it is a must. When the opportunity is presented to learn social dancing, the majority of individuals are interested. This is evidenced by the increasing number of dancing courses offered in the educational program.

There are perhaps two important phases which should be stressed and which are suggested by the term "social dancing". Needless to say, the social aspect of living is one of the major objectives of education, and social dancing has a definite contribution to make in meeting this objective since it gives an opportunity to practice social living. Such factors as contact with individuals, social usage, and recreation of both sexes are part and parcel of any dancing class.

The second phase, dancing, has to do with learning by the individual of the skills of dancing. Many times this is a mechanical process. For many beginners it is a necessary step in order to give the underlying patterns, which in turn will enable them to make such skills their own and will lead to many other creative actions in the area of bodily expression.

In order to dance it is necessary to have as an accompaniment some form of music. Since music is a concomitant part of dance, the appreciation and understanding of certain underlying principles of music should be considered by dancers. In fact, one's ability to interpret music is an underlying factor to success as a dancer. One of the components of music is rhythm. How the individual interprets that rhythm for his individual use in dance is very important. There are always some individuals who readily adapt their bodily actions to rhythm, and there are others who have a great deal of trouble interpreting rhythm. This interpretation of rhythm is particularly important in dancing because of the necessary transmission of rhythm so that partners move in unison.

The relation of music to dance can be illustrated by the fact that the use of just the terms waltz, fox trot, or tango taken out of context may refer either to music or dance.

These factors are not isolated items but are combined to form a whole picture. It may be necessary in the teaching of dancing to deal with the parts, but it should be kept in mind that the integration of the social, skill, and music aspects is of paramount importance.

CHAPTER II
Social Dance Fundamentals

Social dancing is an individual and a cooperative affair. There are many underlying principles of social dancing which are fundamental to performing the skill of dancing. These basic skills have to do with the position of the body, the factors of leading and following, and the conduct of individuals in the dance situation. Many dance instructors overlook these factors and emphasize the importance of performing step patterns. It is true that it is important to stress these step patterns necessary for dancing. However, in addition to teaching the dance movements, the instructor should keep these principles in mind at all times and integrate them with teaching whenever possible. At times it may be desirable to take time out from the teaching of foot patterns and go over some of these principles, but in general they should permeate all of the teaching.

As one increases skillfully in these areas, one becomes a better dancer and is able to enjoy social dancing to the fullest extent. These skills have become so much a part of experienced dancers that they are done unconsciously.

PRINCIPLES

The fundamental principles for dancers are:

1. Good posture is essential for dancers.

2. The eyes should be kept straight ahead, never looking down at the floor or the feet.

3. The head should be held high and chin in with the chest out.

4. There should not be any bends at the neck or waist.

5. Each partner should support his own weight.

6. Dancers should develop a sense of time.

7. Dancing should be done in an easy and graceful manner.

8. Knowledge of step patterns is very important so that it is not necessary to concentrate on dance movements.

9. Step patterns should vary according to the rhythm.

10. Dance in time with the music and on the proper beat.

11. The feet should be kept close together except when taking side steps.

12. The correct social dance position should be taken by the partners.

13. Dance position should be comfortable with the distance between partners not too far or too close.

14. Practice step patterns.

15. Dancing alone will help.

DANCE POSITIONS

There are a number of different social dance positions. However, the two most common positions are known as the closed position, and the open position which is also sometimes called the conversation position.

The closed position, the most commonly used position for dancing, is as follows:

1. In assuming the closed position, the gentleman faces the lady and moves toward her so that she is a few inches to his right.

2. There are some who prefer to have their partner directly in front so that toes are opposite each other. However, many prefer to have the gentleman's right foot between his partner's feet and the left foot outside of his partner's right foot.

3. The gentleman places his right hand firmly below the lady's shoulder blade or on the middle of the back. The fingers are held in a natural closed position. The right elbow is held in a graceful manner at a medium height.

4. The gentleman's left arm is raised so that the elbow is carried away from the body in curved fashion. This gives the effect of being in balance with the right elbow. The fingers are held together with the thumb separated. The hand is tilted so that the palm slightly faces the floor.

5. The lady places her left hand on her partner's right shoulder. With her hand in this position, the left arm follows the lines of her partner's right arm. The lady should not apply downward pressure with her left arm, but just make contact with her partner's right arm so that she can pick up the movements of her partner.

4

6. The lady places her right hand in her partner's left hand so that her little finger curves around the base of the index finger of her partner, and her thumb curves around the base of the thumb of her partner.

7. The lady should hold her right arm up so that her partner does not have to support the weight of the arm.

8. Each should look over his partner's right shoulder.

The open position, the second most important dance position, is as follows:

1. In assuming the open position, the partners stand side by side so that the right side of the gentleman's body is next to the left side of the lady's body.

2. The gentleman's right arm is in the same position as in the closed position with the exception of an outward rotation of the upper arm.

3. The lady's left arm is in the same position as in the closed position with just a slight adjustment for the open position.

4. The gentleman's left arm and the lady's right arm do not change position other than to permit the left shoulder of the gentleman and the right shoulder of the lady to move backward.

5. The open position may vary from the closed position to a quarter turn by each of the partners.

6. The gentleman steps on the left foot or the outside foot while the lady steps on the right foot or the outside foot.

7. When the gentleman steps on the right foot or the inside foot, the lady steps on the left foot or the inside foot.

8. A variation of the open position calls for a dropping of the gentleman's left arm and the lady's right arm. This is sometime called the conversation position.

LEADING

The fundamental essentials for leading are:

1. Assume and hold the proper dance position with your partner.

2. Do not hold your partner too tightly. On the other hand, your partner should not be held too loosely.

3. The gentleman must support his weight so that he is never off balance.

4. Listen to the music and identify the rhythm before starting to dance.

5. Pick up the beat of the rhythm and start dancing on the beat.

6. Step patterns must be learned thoroughly.

7. The step pattern should be executed neatly and precisely.

8. Each step taken must be taken in a definite manner without hesitation.

9. Execute your steps in a confident manner.

10. Start dancing using simple steps before trying intricate or fancy steps.

11. The lead should be the result of entire body movement and not obvious and unrelated motions.

12. Gentleman does not count or give his lead verbally.

Although a gentleman's lead is an outgrowth of proper execution of step and proper body alignment, there are certain parts of the body which will assist in giving the proper lead.

As the step pattern is executed, the upper part of the body reflects the movement. If the step is forward, a pressure is created which indicates to his partner that she should move backward. If the step is backward, the pressure against the partner is reduced indicating that she moves forward.

The right hand holding firmly below the lady's shoulder blade assists in giving the lead.

As the step pattern is executed, the right hand and arm reflect the movement. If the step is forward, the pressure on the partner is reduced indicating that she must move backward. Failure to do this results in the gentleman's loss of his lead. If the step is backward, a pressure is created which indicates to his partner that she must move forward.

The left hand does not play a prominent part in leading. However, it is important that the hand and arm be held in proper dance position. The left hand should reflect the body movements.

In indicating turns, the shoulders twist toward the direction to which the turn is to be made. For right turns, the shoulders twist toward the right; for left turns, the shoulders twist toward the left. This twisting or turning of the shoulders precedes the first step of the turn pattern.

To indicate the lead for the open position the gentleman applies pressure on his partner's back with his arm and turns a quarter turn to his left.

To indicate a movement sideward, the shoulder in the direction of movement is lowered. When moving to the left, the left shoulder is lowered; when moving to the right, the right shoulder is lowered.

FOLLOWING

The fundamental essentials for following are:

1. Hold and maintain proper dance position with your partner. Avoid fancy or unusual holds on your partner.

2. The lady's body weight should be distributed so that her partner does not have to carry her weight.

3. The lady places her left hand on her partner's right shoulder in a firm manner.

4. The lady's right hand and arm are held in position without relying on her partner for support.

5. The lady should maintain her balance allowing her partner's lead to indicate movement.

6. A knowledge and ability to perform basic and intricate step patterns will improve ability to follow.

7. Knowing the man's part gives an appreciation for his part.

8. The lady moves backward from the hip with the toes leading.

9. Dancing with your partner makes you a lighter dancer than if you moved after him.

10. Do not place your foot on the floor until you are ready to place your weight on it.

11. Always be ready for the next step so that the movement is continuous rather than jerky or abrupt.

12. Do not allow yourself to slump or relax to the extreme so that you become heavy.

13. Give yourself a lift and be yourself.

DANCE ETIQUETTE

In social dancing many people are careless about social habits. In order to make dancing a more enjoyable pastime, there are a few fundamental principles of etiquette which when put into practice lend a great deal to the enjoyment of dancing. It cannot be taken for granted that these rules of etiquette are known by all, and therefore it becomes necessary to call attention to these principles.

1. If there is a hostess or receiving line, the dancers should greet the hostess upon arriving at the dance.

2. A gentleman should always dance with the hostess sometime during the evening.

3. A gentleman in the stag line shows his desire to dance with a lady by tapping her partner on the left shoulder.

4. When cutting in the gentleman asks, "May I cut in?", or "May we cut in?". The reply should be, "Certainly". The gentleman then relinquishes the young lady with whom he has been dancing and thanks her for the dance.

5. A gentleman never refuses to relinquish his partner.

6. A lady never refuses to accept an invitation to dance with a gentleman or exchange partners.

7. A gentleman in relinquishing a lady always turns to her and thanks her for the dance.

8. A lady never thanks her partner for a dance but it is permissible to tell him that she enjoyed the dance.

9. After one has been "cut", it is not proper to cut back immediately on the man with whom an exchange of partners has been made.

10. A lady should not be left standing in the middle of the dance floor by herself.

11. A gentleman is responsible to see that his partner enjoys the dance.

CHAPTER III
Fox Trot

The fox trot is the most popular of all dances. The music is written in 4/4 time which indicates that there are four quarter notes to a measure of music. Each quarter note receives one beat. The first and third beats of every measure are accented.

The typical rhythm of fox trot music is represented by the following pattern:

TIME: S QQ   S   S   QQ S

MUSIC COUNT: 1 2 3 4 1 2 3 4 1 2 3 4

TEMPO: 30-48 measures per minute

In fox trot music there is a pulse on the first and third note of every measure.

In the slow fox trots, the first and third notes are not so pronounced.

In the snappy fox trots, there is a light after beat on the second and the fourth note.

All fox trot rhythms are the same, but it is usually recognized that there are various tempos of fox trot, mainly slow, medium, and fast.

When a person dances the fox trot, it is usually thought that he is doing a series of slow and quick steps. A slow step requires the same amount of time as two quick steps, so that in one measure of fox trot music a person may either take four quick steps, two quick steps and one slow step, or two slow steps.

In addition to the various fox trot steps, there are other styles of dancing done to fox trot rhythms which are very popular. These are Jitterbug, Shag, and Charleston which are done to lively and syncopated fox trot rhythms. The steps of these dances are characterized by a definite foot movement which may be evidenced by a complete change of weight, by a kick, by a quick change of the feet done in sequence, by springy steps, or by combinations of these that will form a desired foot pattern.

BASIC FOX TROT STEP
(Box)

Step Pattern	Dance Movement	Time	Dance Count	Measure	Music Count	
1.	Step forward on left foot.	Slow	1, 2	1	1, 2	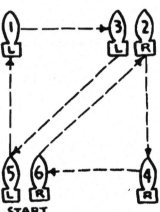
2.	Step diagonally forward on right foot.	Quick	3		3	
3.	Close left foot up to right foot.	Quick	4		4	
4.	Step backward on right foot.	Slow	1, 2	2	1, 2	
5.	Step diagonally backward on left foot.	Quick	3		3	
6.	Close right foot up to left foot.	Quick	4		4	

BASIC FOX TROT STEP
(Forward)

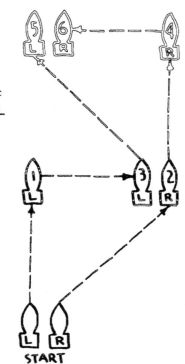

Step Pattern	Dance Movement	Time	Dance Count	Measure	Music Count
1.	Step forward on left foot.	Slow	1, 2	1	1, 2
2.	Step diagonally forward on right foot.	Quick	3		3
3.	Close left foot up to right foot.	Quick	4		4
4.	Step forward on right foot.	Slow	1, 2	2	1, 2
5.	Step diagonally forward on left foot.	Quick	3		3
6.	Close right foot up to left foot.	Quick	4		4

BASIC FOX TROT STEP
(Backward)

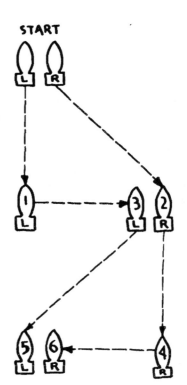

Step Pattern	Dance Movement	Time	Dance Count	Measure	Music Count
1.	Step backward on left foot.	Slow	1, 2	1	1, 2
2.	Step diagonally backward on right foot.	Quick	3		3
3.	Close left foot up to right foot.	Quick	4		4
4.	Step backward on right foot.	Slow	1, 2	2	1, 2
5.	Step diagonally backward on left foot.	Quick	3		3
6.	Close right foot up to left foot.	Quick	4		4

10

FOX TROT STEP
(Variation)
(Forward)

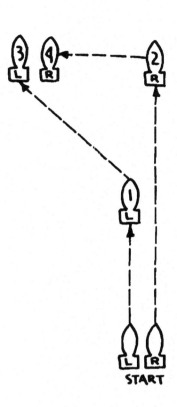

Step Pattern	Dance Movement	Time	Dance Count	Measure*	Music Count
1.	Step forward on left foot.	Slow	1, 2	1	1, 2
2.	Step forward on right foot.	Slow	3, 4		3, 4
3.	Step diagonally forward on left foot.	Quick	1	2	1
4.	Close right foot up to left foot.	Quick	2		2

* This fox trot step takes one and a half measures of music, as do all the fox trot steps that follow.

FOX TROT STEP .
(Variation)
(Backward)

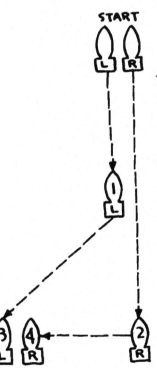

Step Pattern	Dance Movement	Time	Dance Count	Measure	Music Count
1.	Step backward on left foot.	Slow	1, 2	1	1, 2
2.	Step backward on right foot.	Slow	3, 4		3, 4
3.	Step diagonally backward on left foot.	Quick	1	2	1
4.	Close right foot up to left foot.	Quick	2		2

11

FOX TROT STEP
(Variation)
(Side Step)

Step Pattern	Dance Movement	Time	Dance Count	Measure	Music Count	
1.	Step in place on left foot.	Slow	1, 2	1	1, 2	
2.	Step in place on right foot.	Slow	3, 4		3, 4	
3.	Step to the left on left foot.	Quick	1	2	1	
4.	Step to the left on right foot.	Quick	2		2	

FOX TROT STEP
(Variation)
(Open Position)

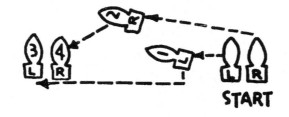

Step Pattern	Dance Movement	Time	Dance Count	Measure	Music Count
1.	Step to left on left foot.	Slow	1, 2	1	1, 2
2.	Step across in front of left foot on right foot.	Slow	3, 4		3, 4
3.	Step to left on left foot.	Quick	1	2	1
4.	Close right foot up to left foot.	Quick	2		2

12

FOX TROT
(Dip)

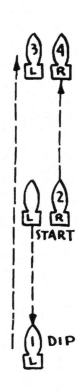

Step Pattern	Dance Movement	Time	Dance Count	Measure	Music Count
1.	Step backward on left foot and dip. (The dip is done by bending left knee slightly to create a swaying motion. Extend right foot forward, raising it off the floor.)	Slow	1, 2	1	1, 2
2.	Step forward on right foot.	Slow	3, 4		3, 4
3.	Step forward on left foot.	Quick	1	2	1
4.	Close right foot up to left foot.	Quick	2		2

JITTERBUG STEP
(Basic)

(Gentleman's Part)

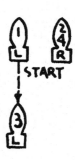

Step Pattern	Dance Movement	Time	Dance Count	Measure	Music Count
1.	Step on left foot.	Slow	1, 2	1	1, 2
2.	Step on right foot.	Slow	3, 4		3, 4
3.	Step back on left foot.	Quick	1	2	1
4.	Step on right foot.	Quick	2		2

13

JITTERBUG STEP
(Basic)

(Lady's Part)

As the gentleman does the basic jitterbug step, the lady is pushed away from him rather than stepping in the same direction. This creates a separation of partners. This separation is a characteristic movement of jitterbug.

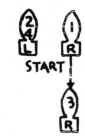

Step Pattern	Dance Movement	Time	Dance Count	Measure	Music Count
1.	Step on right foot.	Slow	1, 2	1	1, 2
2.	Step on left foot.	Slow	3, 4		3, 4
3.	Step back on right foot.	Quick	1	2	1
4.	Step on left foot.	Quick	2		2

JITTERBUG STEP
(Turn Back)

(Gentleman's Part)

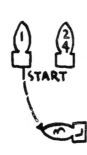

Step Pattern	Dance Movement	Time	Dance Count	Measure	Music Count
1.	Step on left foot.	Slow	1, 2	1	1, 2
2.	Step on right foot.	Slow	3, 4		3, 4
3.	Step back on left foot, and at the same time do a quarter turn counter-clockwise.	Quick	1	2	1
4.	Step on right foot, and at the same time do a quarter turn clockwise.	Quick	2		2

JITTERBUG STEP
(Turn Back)
(Lady's Part)

As the gentleman does the jitterbug step, turn back, the lady's part is different in that she does not advance towards him but is turned back away from him as he turns back. As the gentleman steps back and does a quarter turn counterclockwise on the left foot, the lady steps back and does a quarter turn clockwise on the right foot.

The lady's foot pattern for the turn back step is as follows:

Step Pattern	Dance Movement	Time	Dance Count	Measure	Music Count
1.	Step on right foot.	Slow	1, 2	1	1, 2
2.	Step on left foot.	Slow	3, 4		3, 4
3.	Step back on right foot, and at the same time do a quarter turn clockwise.	Quick	1	2	1
4.	Step on left foot, and at the same time do a quarter turn counter-clockwise.	Quick	2		2

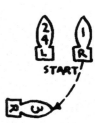

JITTERBUG STEP
(Clockwise Turn for Gentlemen)

Step Pattern	Dance Movement	Time	Dance Count	Measure	Music Count
1.	Step diagonally left forward on left foot, and at the same time do a half turn clockwise. (1 A and 1 B)	Slow	1, 2	1	1, 2
2.	Step on right foot.	Slow	3, 4		3, 4
3.	Step back on left foot.	Quick	1	2	1
4.	Step on right foot.	Quick	2		2

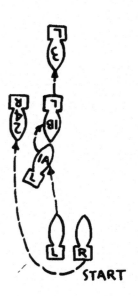

JITTERBUG STEP
(Clockwise Turn for Ladies)

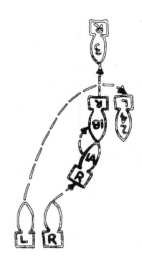

Step Pattern	Dance Movement	Time	Dance Count	Measure	Music Count
1.	Step diagonally right forward on right foot, and at the same time do a half turn clockwise. (1A and 1B)	Slow	1, 2	1	1, 2
2.	Step on left foot.	Slow	3, 4		3, 4
3.	Step back on right foot.	Quick	1	2	1
4.	Step on left foot.	Quick	2		2

JITTERBUG STEP
(Counterclockwise Turn for Gentlemen)

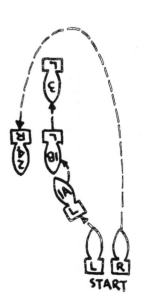

Step Pattern	Dance Movement	Time	Dance Count	Measure	Music Count
1.	Step diagonally left forward on left foot, and at the same time do a half turn counterclockwise. (1A and 1B)	Slow	1, 2	1	1, 2
2.	Step on right foot.	Slow	3, 4		3, 4
3.	Step back on left foot.	Quick	1	2	1
4.	Step on right foot.	Quick	2		2

16

JITTERBUG STEP
(Counterclockwise Turn for Ladies)

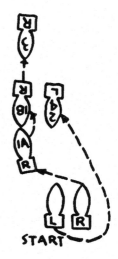

Step Pattern	Dance Movement	Time	Dance Count	Measure	Music Count
1.	Step diagonally left forward on right foot, and at the same time do a half turn counterclockwise. (1A and 1B)	Slow	1, 2	1	1, 2
2.	Step on left foot.	Slow	3, 4		3, 4
3.	Step back on right foot.	Quick	1		1
4.	Step on left foot.	Quick	2		2

SINGLE LINDY
(Gentleman's Part)

Step Pattern	Dance Movement	Time	Dance Count	Measure	Music Count
1.	Step left sideward on left foot.	Slow	1	1	1, 2
2.	Step left sideward on right foot.		2		
3.	Step on left foot.		3		
4.	Step right sideward on right foot.	Slow	1		3, 4
5.	Step right sideward on left foot.		2		
6.	Step on right foot.		3		
7.	Step back on left foot.	Quick	1	2	1
8.	Step on right foot.	Quick	2		2

SINGLE LINDY
(Lady's Part)

Step Pattern	Dance Movement	Time	Dance Count	Measure	Music Count
1.	Step right sideward on right foot.		1	1	
2.	Step right sideward on left foot.	Slow	2		1, 2
3.	Step on right foot.		3		
4.	Step left sideward on left foot.		1		
5.	Step left sideward on right foot.	Slow	2		3, 4
6.	Step on left foot.		3		
7.	Step back on right foot.	Quick	1	2	1
8.	Step on left foot.	Quick	2		2

SHAG

Step Pattern	Dance Movement	Time	Dance Count	Measure	Music Count
1.	Step across and in front of left foot on right foot.	Slow	Step	1	1, 2
2.	Step on left foot.		1		
3.	Step on right foot.	Slow	2		3, 4
4.	Step on left foot.		3		
5.	Kick with right foot.	Quick	Kick	2	1
6.	Step on right foot.	Quick	1		2
7.	Step on left foot.		2		

Note: The lady and the gentleman follow the identical step pattern. The dance position for this shag calls for the gentleman to hold the lady's right hand with his left hand and the lady's left hand with his right hand.

THE SHAG TURN
(Clockwise)

Step Pattern	Dance Movement	Time	Dance Count	Measure	Music Count
1.	Step across and in front of left foot on right foot, and do a half turn clockwise. (1A and 1B)	Slow	Step	1	1, 2
2.	Step on left foot.		1		
3.	Step on right foot.	Slow	2		3, 4
4.	Step on left foot.		3		
5.	Kick with right foot.	Quick	Kick	2	1
6.	Step on right foot.	Quick	1		
7.	Step on left foot.		2		2

THE SHAG TURN
(Counterclockwise)

Step Pattern	Dance Movement	Time	Dance Count	Measure	Music Count
1.	Step across and in front of left foot on right foot, and do a half turn counterclockwise. (1A and 1B)	Slow	Step	1	1, 2
2.	Step on left foot.		1		
3.	Step on right foot.	Slow	2		3, 4
4.	Step on left foot.		3		
5.	Kick with right foot.	Quick	Kick	2	1
6.	Step on right foot.	Quick	1		2
7.	Step on left foot.		2		

19

TIME SHAG

Step Pattern	Dance Movement	Time	Dance Count	Measure	Music Count
1.	Step, hop on left foot.	Slow	1, 2	1	1, 2
2.	Step, hop on right foot.	Slow	3, 4		3, 4
3.	Step on left foot.	Quick	1	2	1
4.	Step on right foot.	Quick	2		2

TIME SHAG
(Variation)

Step Pattern	Dance Movement	Time	Dance Count	Measure	Music Count
1.	Step on left foot and hold.	Slow	1, hold	1	1, 2
2.	Step on right foot and hold.	Slow	2, hold		3, 4
3.	Step on left foot.				
4.	Step on right foot.	Slow	1, 2, 3	2	1, 2
5.	Step on left foot.				
6.	Step on right foot and hold.	Slow	4, hold		3, 4

Note: This fox trot step takes two measures of music to complete.

CHARLESTON

START

Step Pattern	Dance Movement	Time	Dance Count	Measure	Music Count
1.	Turn on balls of feet so that the heels are apart, with the right heel off the floor.	Quick	1	1	1
2.	Turn on ball of the left foot so that the left heel is inward and step forward with the right foot, touching the ball of the right foot with heel inward and lifted off the floor.	Quick	2		2
3.	Turn on balls of feet so that the heels are apart, with the right heel off the floor.	Quick	3		3
4.	Turn on the ball of the left foot so that the heel is inward and step backward with the right foot with heels inward.	Quick	4		4
5.	Turn on balls of feet so that the heels are apart, with the left heel off the floor.	Quick	5	2	1
6.	Turn on the ball of the right foot so that the right heel is inward and step backward with the left foot, with heel inward and lifted off the floor.	Quick	6		2
7.	Turn on balls of feet so that the heels are apart, with the left heel off the floor.	Quick	7		3
8.	Turn on ball of right foot so that the heel is inward and step forward with the left foot so that the heels are inward.	Quick	8		4

21

CHARLESTON SWING

KICK

START

Step Pattern	Dance Movement	Time	Dance Count	Measure	Music Count
1.	Step forward on left foot.	Slow	1, 2	1	1, 2
2.	Swing right foot forward and kick.	Slow	3, 4		3, 4
3.	Step backward on right foot.	Slow	5, 6	2	1, 2
4.	Place left foot backward, touching ball of left foot to floor.	Slow	7, 8		3, 4

CHAPTER IV
Waltz

The waltz is one of the older dances and although it is not as popular as the fox trot, it still has wide appeal as a social dance. Perhaps the reason for this is that the variety of step patterns in the waltz are not as well known as those of the fox trot.

The modern waltz is of a slow tempo and provides the opportunity for a wide range of step patterns and combinations. The faster tempo waltz, called the Viennese Waltz, does not permit the variations other than continuous right and left turns. Whether it be a slow or fast waltz, the three movements of the basic waltz step blend perfectly with the beat of each measure.

Waltz music is written in 3/4 time which indicates that there are three quarter notes to a measure of music. Each quarter note receives one beat. In the waltz, the accent is on the first beat of each measure of music.

The typical rhythm of waltz music is represented by the following pattern:

WALTZ

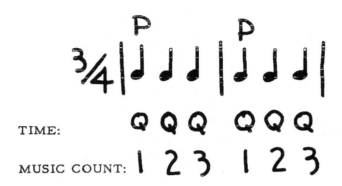

TIME:

MUSIC COUNT: 1 2 3 1 2 3

TEMPO: 30-60 measures per minute

BASIC WALTZ STEP
(Box)

Step Pattern	Dance Movement	Time	Dance Count	Measure	Music Count
1.	Step forward on left foot.	Quick	1	1	1
2.	Step diagonally forward on right foot.	Quick	2		2
3.	Close left foot up to right foot.	Quick	3		3
4.	Step backward on right foot.	Quick	1	2	1
5.	Step diagonally backward on left foot.	Quick	2		2
6.	Close right foot up to left foot.	Quick	3		3

24

BASIC WALTZ STEP
(Forward)

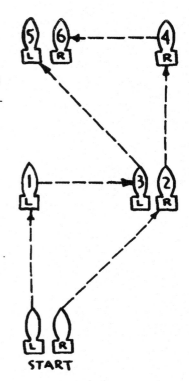

Step Pattern	Dance Movement	Time	Dance Count	Measure	Music Count
1.	Step forward on left foot.	Quick	1	1	1
2.	Step diagonally forward on right foot.	Quick	2		2
3.	Close left foot up to right foot.	Quick	3		3
4.	Step forward on right foot.	Quick	1	2	1
5.	Step diagonally forward on left foot.	Quick	2		2
6.	Close right foot up to left foot.	Quick	3		3

BASIC WALTZ STEP
(Backward)

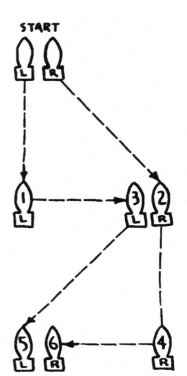

Step Pattern	Dance Movement	Time	Dance Count	Measure	Music Count
1.	Step backward on left foot.	Quick	1	1	1
2.	Step diagonally backward on right foot.	Quick	2		2
3.	Close left foot up to right foot.	Quick	3		3
4.	Step backward on right foot.	Quick	1	2	1
5.	Step diagonally backward on left foot.	Quick	2		2
6.	Close right foot up to left foot.	Quick	3		3

BASIC WALTZ STEP
(Left Turn)

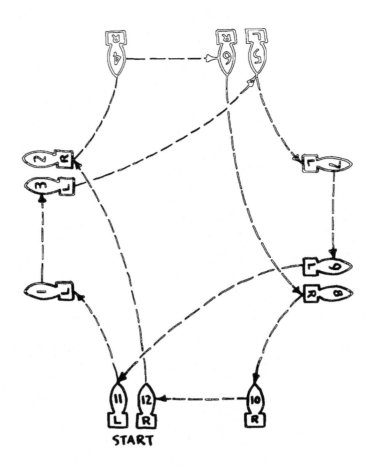

START

Step Pattern	Dance Movement	Time	Dance Count	Measure	Music Count
1.	Step forward with left foot, turning a quarter turn to the left.	Quick	1	1	1
2.	Step forward with right foot, placing it parallel to the left foot.	Quick	2		2
3.	Close left foot up to right foot.	Quick	3		3
4.	Step backward with right foot, turning a quarter turn to the left.	Quick	1	2	1
5.	Step backward with left foot, placing it parallel to the right foot.	Quick	2		2
6.	Close right foot up to left foot.	Quick	3		3

26

BASIC WALTZ STEP (Continued)

Step Pattern	Dance Movement	Time	Dance Count	Measure	Music Count
7.	Step forward with left foot, turning a quarter turn to the left.	Quick	1	3	1
8.	Step forward with right foot, placing it parallel to the left foot.	Quick	2		2
9.	Close left foot up to right foot.	Quick	3		3
10.	Step backward with right foot, turning a quarter turn to the left.	Quick	1	4	1
11.	Step backward with left foot, placing it parallel to the right foot.	Quick	2		2
12.	Close right foot up to left foot.	Quick	3		3

BASIC WALTZ STEP
(Right Turn)

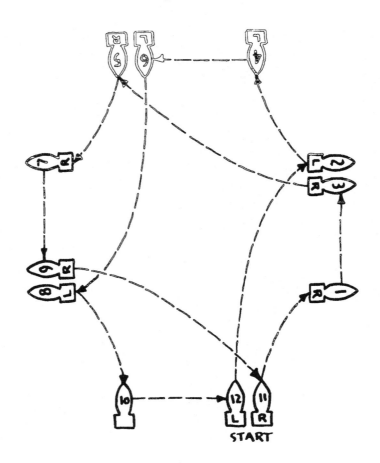

Step Pattern	Dance Movement	Time	Dance Count	Measure	Music Count
1.	Step forward with right foot, turning a quarter turn to the right.	Quick	1	1	1
2.	Step forward with left foot, placing it parallel to the right foot.	Quick	2		2
3.	Close right foot up to the left foot.	Quick	3		3
4.	Step backward with left foot, turning a quarter turn to the right.	Quick	1	2	1
5.	Step backward with right foot, placing it parallel to the left foot.	Quick	2		2
6.	Draw left foot up to the right foot.	Quick	3		3

BASIC WALTZ STEP (Continued)

Step Pattern	Dance Movement	Time	Dance Count	Measure	Music Count
7.	Step forward with right foot, turning a quarter turn to the right.	Quick	1	3	1
8.	Step forward with left foot, placing it parallel to the right foot.	Quick	2		2
9.	Close right foot up to the left foot.	Quick	3		3
10.	Step backward with left foot, turning a quarter turn to the right.	Quick	1	4	1
11.	Step backward with right foot, placing it parallel to the left foot.	Quick	2		2
12.	Close left foot up to the right foot.	Quick	3		3

HESITATION WALTZ STEP
(Forward and Backward)

Step Pattern	Dance Movement	Time	Dance Count	Measure	Music Count
1.	Step forward on left foot.	Quick	1	1	1
2.	Point right foot to the right side of the left foot, keeping weight on the left foot.	Quick	2		2
3.	Continue to hold position 2.	Quick	3		3
4.	Step backward on right foot.	Quick	1	2	1
5.	Point left toe to the left side of the right foot, keeping weight on right foot.	Quick	2		2
6.	Continue to hold position 5.	Quick	3		3

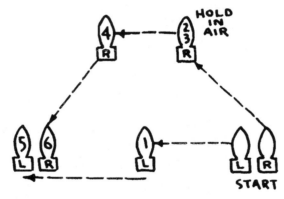

HESITATION WALTZ STEP
(Side)

Step Pattern	Dance Movement	Time	Dance Count	Measure	Music Count
1.	Make a quarter turn to the left, step on the left foot.	Quick	1	1	1
2.	Swing right foot across, holding this foot in the air.	Quick	2		2
3.	Continue to hold position 2.	Quick	3		3
4.	Step left sidewards on right foot.	Quick	1	2	1
5.	Step left sidewards on left foot.	Quick	2		2
6.	Close right foot to left foot.	Quick	3		3

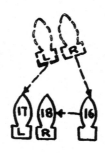

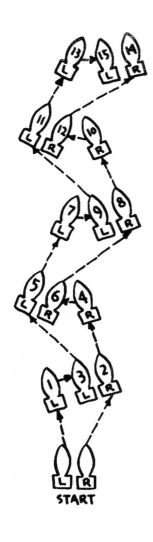

START

ENTRANCE PATTERN

SERPENTINE WALTZ

Step Pattern	Dance Movement	Time	Dance Count	Measure	Music Count
1.	Step diagonally forward on left foot.	Quick	1	1	1
2.	Step diagonally forward on right foot.	Quick	2		2
3.	Close left foot up to right foot.	Quick	3		3
	Note: On the 2nd and 3rd step the man turns his partner so that her right shoulder is next to his right shoulder.				
4.	Step forward on right foot.	Quick	1	2	1
5.	Step diagonally left forward on left foot.	Quick	2		2
6.	Close right foot up to left.	Quick	3		3
	Note: On the 5th and 6th step the man turns his partner so that her left shoulder is next to his left shoulder.				
7.	Step forward on left foot.	Quick	1	3	1
8.	Step diagonally right forward on right foot.	Quick	2		2
9.	Close left foot up to right.	Quick	3		3
	Note: On the 8th and 9th step the man turns his partner so that her right shoulder is next to his right shoulder.				
10.	Step forward on right foot.	Quick	1	4	1
11.	Step diagonally left forward on left foot.	Quick	2		2

31

Step Pattern	Dance Movement	Time	Dance Count	Measure	Music Count
12.	Close right foot up to left.	Quick	3		3
	Note: On the 11th and 12th step the man turns his partner so that her left shoulder is next to his left shoulder.				
13.	Step forward on the left foot.	Quick	1	5	1
14.	Step diagonally right forward on right foot.	Quick	2		2
15.	Close left foot up to right foot.	Quick	3		3
	Note: On the 14th and 15th step the man turns his partner so that her right shoulder is next to his right shoulder.				
16.	Step diagonally backward on right foot.	Quick	1	6	1
17.	Step diagonally backward on left foot.	Quick	2		2
18.	Close right foot up to left foot.	Quick	3		3
	Note: This returns dancers to closed position.				

EXIT PATTERN

CHAPTER V
Tango

The tango was the first Latin-American dance to attain popularity in this country. The music is written in 2/4 time and each beat of the measure is equally stressed. The dance is based on two slow steps to each measure of music.

The typical rhythm of tango music is represented by the following pattern:

TIME: S QQ S S QQ S
MUSIC COUNT: 1 + 2 + 1 + 2 + 1 + 2 +

TEMPO: 40-50 measures per minute

In the tango, proficiency in the style of movement peculiar to this type of dance is very important. The tango could be described as a "cat-like" walk. This appearance is obtained by doing the step slowly and deliberately. Superfluous movement above the hip-line should be avoided, at the same time avoiding the impression of being stiff. It is a smooth, plastic dance but it lacks the freedom and non-restraint of the fox trot and the waltz. The appearance of dignity and restraint is attained by careful correlation of movement.

The manner of stepping in the tango must be distinctive. It is made with the same decision that is used in walking. By placing your foot in this manner, greater use may be made of the knee joint and it creates the effect of lifting the foot from the floor.

BASIC TANGO STEP

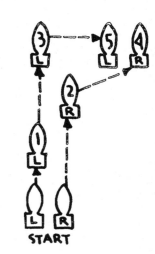

Step Pattern	Dance Movement	Time	Dance Count	Measure	Music Count
1.	Step forward on left foot.	Slow	1-&	1	1-&
2.	Step forward on right foot.	Slow	2-&		2-&
3.	Step forward on left foot.	Quick	1	2	1
4.	Step diagonally forward on right foot.	Quick	&		&
5.	Close left foot up to right foot, keeping the weight on the right foot.	Slow	2-&		2-&

TANGO DIP

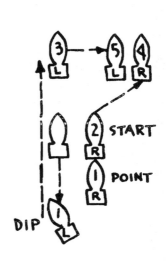

Step Pattern	Dance Movement	Time	Dance Count	Measure	Music Count
1.	Step backward on left foot and dip. (The dip is done by bending left knee slightly. Turn left toe out so that when bending the knee it will avoid contact with partner's knee.)	Slow	1-&	1	1-&
2.	Step forward on right foot.	Slow	2-&		2-&
3.	Step forward on left foot.	Quick	1	2	1
4.	Step diagonally forward on right foot.	Quick	&		&
5.	Close left foot up to right foot, keeping the weight on the right foot.	Slow	2-&		2-&

TANGO CROSS STEP

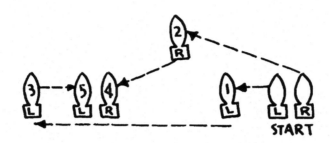

Step Pattern	Dance Movement	Time	Dance Count	Measure	Music Count
1.	Step sideward on left foot.	Slow	1-&	1	1-&
2.	Cross right foot in front left foot.	Slow	2-&		2-&
3.	Step sideward on left foot.	Quick	1	2	1
4.	Step diagonally back on right foot.	Quick	&		&
5.	Close left foot up to right foot, keeping the weight on the right foot.	Slow	2-&		2-&

TANGO CROSS STEP TURN

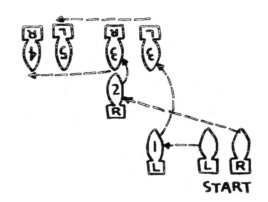

(Gentleman's Part)

Step Pattern	Dance Movement	Time	Dance Count	Measure	Music Count
1.	Step sideward on left foot.	Slow	1-&	1	1-&
2.	Cross right foot in front of left foot.	Slow	2-&		2-&
3.	Pivot on right foot, turning a half turn counterclockwise. Step to the left on left foot.	Quick	1	2	1
4.	Step sideward on right foot.	Quick	&		&
5.	Close left foot up to right foot, keeping the weight on the right foot.	Slow	2-&		2-&

TANGO CROSS STEP TURN

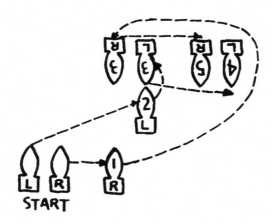

START

(Lady's Part)

Step Pattern	Dance Movement	Time	Dance Count	Measure	Music Count
1.	Step sideward on right foot.	Slow	1-&	1	1-&
2.	Cross left foot in front of right foot.	Slow	2-&		2-&
3.	Pivoting on left foot, the lady is turned by her partner a half turn around him. She then steps to the right on the right foot.	Quick	1	2	1
4.	Step sideward on left foot.	Quick	&		&
5.	Close right foot up to left foot, keeping the weight on the left foot.	Slow	2-&		2-&

TANGO VARIATION

Step Pattern	Dance Movement	Time	Dance Count	Measure	Music Count
1.	Cross left foot behind right foot.	Slow	1-&	1	1-&
2.	Step diagonally backward on right foot.	Quick	2		2
3.	Step diagonally backward on left foot.	Quick	&		&
4.	Cross right foot in front left foot.	Slow	1-&	2	1-&
5.	Step diagonally forward on left foot.	Quick	2		2
6.	Step diagonally forward on right foot.	Quick	&		&
7.	Close left foot up to right foot, keeping the weight on the right foot.	Slow	1-&	3	1-&

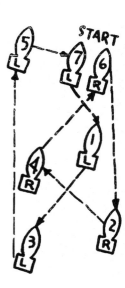

Note: At the end of the basic step, instead of closing the left foot up to the right foot, this tango variation could be started by crossing the left foot behind the right foot on the last movement of the basic step.

38

CHAPTER VI
Rumba

Of all the Latin-American dances, the most popular is the rumba. The background rhythm is given by the claves or sticks, a pair of cylindrical wooden blocks which are hit together; the maracas or rattles, a pair of gourds filled with dry seeds; the guiro or scraper, a serrated calabash; and the bongo, a small wooden drum with a parchment head.

The rumba in this country is in reality the son. Although closely related in character to the rumba, the tempo of the son is much slower; or it may be the danzon, which is a little faster in tempo. We may, therefore, compare the son and danzon to our slow and fast fox trots which are danced in the same manner except for the difference in tempo.

It is characterized by short steps with the feet flat on the floor and accompanied by a subtle swaying of the hips. There is no movement of the upper part of the body in doing the rumba. In the rumba, as the hip is allowed to sway either right or left, the opposite leg is relaxed and the foot is moved into position forward, backward, or sideward. This gives the effect of the hips moving opposite to the stepping leg, instead of toward it as in normal walking and in most dancing. This timing of the feet in the rumba is possible only because the steps are shorter.

The typical rhythm of rumba music is represented by the following patterns:

TIME: Q   Q   S   Q   Q   S

MUSIC COUNT: 1   2   3 4   1   2   3 4

TEMPO: 30-56 measures per minute

The claves click:

The Maracas shake out:

The guiro grates:

Before attempting to learn the rumba steps, the rumba motion should be learned. Sufficient time should be taken to learn this motion.

RUMBA MOTION

1. Shift the weight to the heel of the left foot and allow the right leg to bend. This permits the left hip to be higher than the right hip.

2. Now shift the weight to the heel of the right foot and allow the left leg to bend. This permits the right hip to be higher than the left hip.

3. Again shift the weight to the heel of the left foot and allow the right leg to bend. This permits the left hip to be higher than the right hip. After these three motions, there is a pause.

BASIC RUMBA STEP
(Box)

Step Pattern	Dance Movement	Time	Dance Count	Measure	Music Count
1.	Step left sideward on left foot.	Quick	1	1	1
2.	Close right foot up to left foot.	Quick	2		2
3.	Step forward on left foot.	Quick	3		3
	(Hold position 3.)	Quick	Pause		4
4.	Step diagonally right forward on right foot.	Quick	1	2	1
5.	Close left foot up to right foot.	Quick	2		2
6.	Step backward on right foot.	Quick	3		3
	(Hold position 6.)	Quick	Pause		4

FORWARD WALKING RUMBA STEP

Step Pattern	Dance Movement	Time	Dance Count	Measure	Music Count
1.	Step forward on left foot.	Quick	1	1	1
2.	Step forward on right foot.	Quick	2		2
3.	Step forward on left foot.	Quick	3		3
	(Hold position 3.)	Quick	Pause		4
4.	Step forward on right foot.	Quick	1	2	1
5.	Step forward on left foot.	Quick	2		2
6.	Step forward on right foot.	Quick	3		3
	(Hold position 6.)	Quick	Pause		4

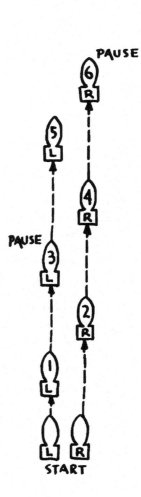

41

BACKWARD WALKING RUMBA STEP

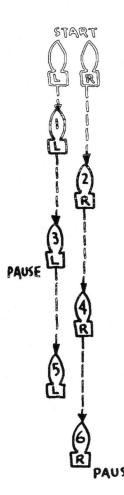

Step Pattern	Dance Movement	Time	Dance Count	Measure	Music Count
1.	Step backward on left foot.	Quick	1	1	1
2.	Step backward on right foot.	Quick	2		2
3.	Step backward on left foot.	Quick	3		3
	(Hold position 3.)	Quick	Pause		4
4.	Step backward on right foot.	Quick	1	2	1
5.	Step backward on left foot.	Quick	2		2
6.	Step backward on right foot.	Quick	3		3
	(Hold position 6.)	Quick	Pause		4

RUMBA VARIATION
(Turn and Walk)

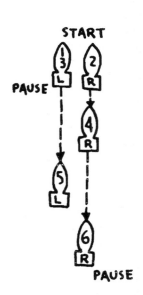

(Gentleman's Part)

Step Pattern	Dance Movement	Time	Dance Count	Measure	Music Count
1.	Step in place on left foot.	Quick	1	1	1
2.	Step in place on right foot.	Quick	2		2
3.	Step in place on left foot.	Quick	3		3
	(Hold position 3.)	Quick	Pause		4
4.	Step backward on right foot.	Quick	1	2	1
5.	Step backward on left foot.	Quick	2		2
6.	Step backward on right foot.	Quick	3		3
	(Hold position 6.)	Quick	Pause		4

RUMBA VARIATION
(Turn and Walk)

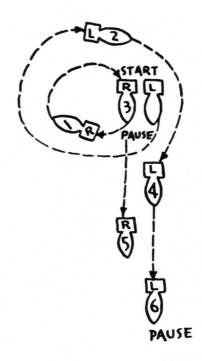

(Lady's Part)

Step Pattern	Dance Movement	Time	Dance Count	Measure	Music Count
1.	Step on right foot starting to make a clockwise turn.	Quick	1	1	1
2.	Step on left foot continuing to make a clockwise turn.	Quick	2		2
3.	Step on right foot completing the clockwise turn, facing partner.	Quick	3		3
	(Hold position 3.)	Quick	Pause		4
4.	Step forward on left foot.	Quick	1	2	1
5.	Step forward on right foot.	Quick	2		2
6.	Step forward on left foot.	Quick	3		3
	(Hold position 6.)	Quick	Pause		4

RUMBA VARIATION
(Wheel)

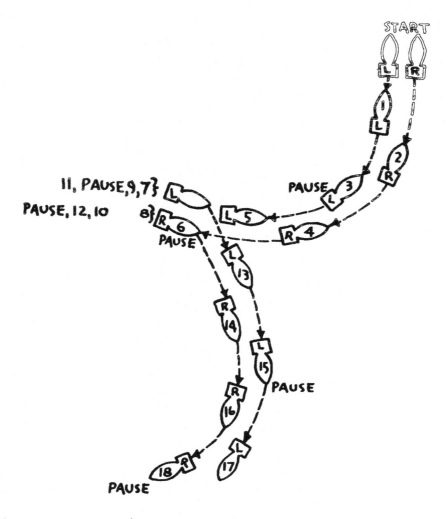

(Gentleman's Part)

Step Pattern	Dance Movement	Time	Dance Count	Measure	Music Count
1.	Step backward on left foot, starting circle with left hand of gentleman and right hand of lady as a pivot point.	Quick	1	1	1
2.	Step backward on right foot, continue circle.	Quick	2		2
3.	Step backward on left foot, continue circle.	Quick	3		3
	(Hold position 3.)	Quick	Pause		4
4.	Step backward on right foot, continue circle.	Quick	1	2	1

RUMBA VARIATION (Continued)

(Gentleman's Part)

Step Pattern	Dance Movement	Time	Dance Count	Measure	Music Count
5.	Step backward on left foot, continue circle.	Quick	2		2
6.	Step backward on right foot, continue circle.	Quick	3		3
	(Hold position 6.)	Quick	Pause		4
7.	Step in place on left foot.	Quick	1	3	1
8.	Step in place on right foot.	Quick	2		2
9.	Step in place on left foot.	Quick	3		3
	(Hold position 9.)				
10.	Step in place on right foot.	Quick	1	4	1
11.	Step in place on left foot.	Quick	2		2
12.	Step in place on right foot.	Quick	3		3
	(Hold position 12.)	Quick	Pause		4
13.	Step forward on left foot. At this point partners have right shoulder to right shoulder. Using right shoulders as a pivot point, each partner moves forward in a clockwise direction.	Quick	1	5	1
14.	Step forward on right foot, continue circle.	Quick	2		2
15.	Step forward on left foot, continue circle.	Quick	3		3
	(Hold position 15.)	Quick	Pause		4
16.	Step forward on right foot, continue circle.	Quick	1	6	1
17.	Step forward on left foot, continue circle.	Quick	2		2
18.	Step forward on right foot. On this step the partners pivot so that they assume a face to face position.	Quick	3		3
	(Hold position 18.)	Quick	4		4

RUMBA VARIATION
(Wheel)

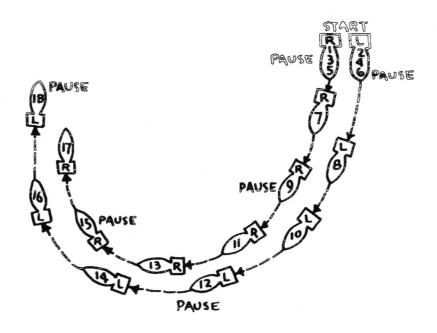

(Lady's Part)

Step Pattern	Dance Movement	Time	Dance Count	Measure	Music Count
1.	Step in place on right foot.	Quick	1	1	1
2.	Step in place on left foot.	Quick	2		2
3.	Step in place on right foot.	Quick	3		3
	(Hold position 3.)	Quick	Pause		4
4.	Step in place on left foot.	Quick	1	2	1
5.	Step in place on right foot.	Quick	2		2
6.	Step in place on left foot.	Quick	3		3
	(Hold position 6.)	Quick	Pause		4
7.	Step forward on right foot, starting circle with left hand of gentleman and right hand of lady as a pivot point.	Quick	1	3	1
8.	Step forward on left foot, continue circle.	Quick	2		2
9.	Step forward on right foot, continue circle.	Quick	3		3

RUMBA VARIATION (Continued)

(Lady's Part)

Step Pattern	Dance Movement	Time	Dance Count	Measure	Music Count
	(Hold position 9.)	Quick	Pause		4
10.	Step forward on left foot, continue circle.	Quick	1	4	1
11.	Step forward on right foot, continue circle.	Quick	2		2
12.	Step forward on left foot, continue circle.	Quick	3		3
	(Hold position 12.)	Quick	Pause		4
13.	Step forward on right foot. At this point partners have right shoulder to right shoulder. Using right shoulders as a pivot point, each partner moves forward in a clockwise direction.	Quick	1	5	1
14.	Step forward on left foot, continue circle.	Quick	2		2
15.	Step forward on right foot, continue circle.	Quick	3		3
	(Hold position 15.)	Quick	Pause		4
16.	Step forward on left foot, continue circle.	Quick	1	6	1
17.	Step forward on right foot, continue circle.	Quick	2		2
18.	Step forward on left foot. On this step the partners pivot so that they assume a face to face position.	Quick	3		3
	(Hold position 18.)	Quick	Pause		4

CHAPTER VII
Conga

The conga is played in rather fast 2/4 time and can be recognized readily by a heavily accented drum beat on every fourth count. Two measures are counted together. In doing the dance step, there are only two steps to a measure of music. The basic conga step requires four counts, or two measures of music.

The typical rhythm of conga music is represented by the following pattern:

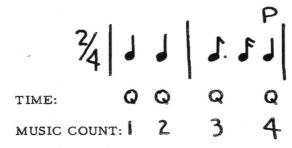

TIME:	Q	Q	Q	Q
MUSIC COUNT:	1	2	3	4

TEMPO: 50-60 measures per minute

48

The basic conga step is three smooth walking steps taken with the feet flat on the floor, followed by an accenting movement on the fourth count. This accented movement is a sideward throw of the hips, accompanied by a quick movement of the leg that has no weight.

To do the conga, take three walking steps and then kick. Then, starting with the free foot, or the foot that has kicked, take three more walking steps and then kick.

A popular way of doing the conga is to form a line, alternating a gentleman and lady, placing hands on the shoulders of the person in front. The line then follows the leader doing the basic conga step.

BASIC CONGA STEP

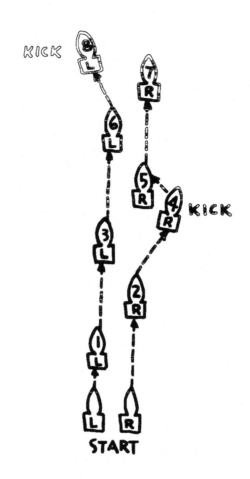

Step Pattern	Dance Movement	Time	Dance Count	Measure	Music Count
1.	Step forward on left foot.	Quick	1	1	1
2.	Step forward on right foot.	Quick	2		2
3.	Step forward on left foot.	Quick	3	2	3
4.	Kick right foot in air.	Quick	Kick		4
5.	Step forward on right foot.	Quick	1	3	1
6.	Step forward on left foot.	Quick	2		2
7.	Step forward on right foot.	Quick	3	4	3
8.	Kick left foot in air.	Quick	Kick		4

50

CONGA SIDE STEP

Step Pattern	Dance Movement	Time	Dance Count	Measure	Music Count
1.	Step to left on left foot.	Quick	1	1	1
2.	Cross right foot in front of left foot.	Quick	2		2
3.	Step left on left foot.	Quick	3	2	3
4.	Kick right foot in air.	Quick	Kick		4

CONGA TURN

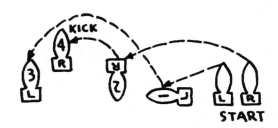

Step Pattern	Dance Movement	Time	Dance Count	Measure	Music Count
1.	Step to left on left foot doing a quarter turn counterclockwise.	Quick	1	1	1
2.	Step to left on right foot doing a quarter turn counterclockwise.	Quick	2		2
3.	Step to left on left foot doing a half turn counter- clockwise.	Quick	3	2	3
4.	Kick right foot in air.	Quick	Kick		4

CHAPTER VIII
Mambo

Mambo music is a certain style of playing popular melodies rather than a musical form. The piano often plays a predominant role in mambo music and it may be described as a "hot style" of playing. The basic melody of the mambo is frequently treated with rhythmic dislocations and syncopations. Due to the rhythmic dislocations of mambo music, it becomes very important for the dancers to maintain a consistent rhythm. It has a wide range of tempos similar to other dances, ranging from slow to fast.

In dancing the mambo arms, legs, hips, and heads are thrown around as the dancer and his partner assume that they are the only two people on the floor. With many dancers there is no restrained movement in the mambo, or any inhibitions. It is described as sexy, wild, and grotesque. However, if the mambo is to maintain its popularity, the extreme characteristics of its movements will have to be smoothed out and done with ease and in simple dance style.

The typical rhythm of mambo music is represented by the following pattern:

TIME: S   Q Q   S   Q Q

MUSIC COUNT: 1 2 3 4   1 2 3 4

TEMPO: 30-50 measure per minute.

The Claves click:

The Bass slaps:

53

BASIC MAMBO STEP

Step Pattern	Dance Movement	Time	Dance Count	Measure	Music Count
1.	Step forward on left foot.	Slow	1, 2	1	1, 2
2.	Step forward on right foot.	Quick	3		3
3.	Step in place on left foot.	Quick	4		4
4.	Step backward on right foot.	Slow	1, 2	2	1, 2
5.	Step backward on left foot.	Quick	3		3
6.	Step in place on right foot.	Quick	4		4

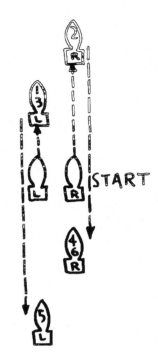

MAMBO VARIATION

Step Pattern	Dance Movement	Time	Dance Count	Measure	Music Count
1.	Step forward on left foot.	Slow	1, 2	1	1, 2
2.	Step diagonally right on right foot.	Quick	3		3
3.	Step in place on left foot.	Quick	4		4
4.	Close right foot up to left foot.	Slow	1, 2	2	1, 2
5.	Step sideward on left foot.	Quick	3		3
6.	Step in place on right foot.	Quick	4		4

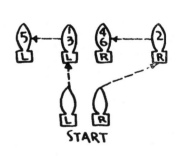

CHAPTER IX
Samba

The samba is the liveliest of the ballroom dances introduced from Latin America. The tempo is rather fast and the mood quite gay.

The step is very light and springy and done on the balls of the feet. In doing the basic step, the body rocks. In doing the step forward, the head and trunk lean backward. In doing the step backward, the head and trunk lean forward. The hands help to accentuate this rocking movement of the body.

The basic step is very much like the waltz. However, there is a double rise and fall within the 2/4 measure of samba music, while in the waltz there is a single rise and fall within 3/4 measure.

The typical rhythm of samba music is represented by the following pattern:

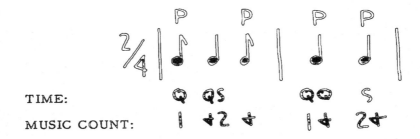

TIME: Q QS   QQ S

MUSIC COUNT: 1 &2 &   1& 2&

TEMPO: Usually 60 measures per minute

    The basic rhythm of the samba is illustrated by the first measure above, and is either combined or repeated with the rhythm of the second measure.

BASIC SAMBA

Step Pattern	Dance Movement	Time	Dance Count	Measure	Music Count
1.	Step forward on left foot.	Quick	1	1	1
2.	Close right foot up to left foot.	Quick	&		&
3.	Step in place on left foot.	Slow	2-&		2-&
4.	Step backward on right foot.	Quick	1	2	1
5.	Close left foot back to right foot.	Quick	&		&
6.	Step in place on right foot.	Slow	2-&		2-&

    There is a characteristic rocking movement of the body forward and backward. Steps 1, 2, and 3 the head and trunk lean backward. Steps 4, 5, and 6 the head and trunk lean forward.

NOTE: In the samba the pause is on dance movement 3 and dance movement 6.

SAMBA
(Walking Step)

Step Pattern	Dance Movement	Time	Dance Count	Measure	Music Count
1.	Step forward on left foot.	Quick	1	1	1
2.	Step in place on ball of right foot.	Quick	&		&
3.	Step in place on left foot.	Slow	2-&		2-&
4.	Step forward on right foot.	Quick	1	2	1
5.	Step in place on ball of left foot.	Quick	&		&
6.	Step forward on right foot.	Slow	2-&		2-&

<u>Note</u>: Dance movements 1 and 2, and 4 and 5 are done as a rocking movement forward and backward.

Partners assume an open position so that the right side of the gentleman and the left side of the lady are next to each other. Both partners progress forward.

As the step forward is made on the left foot, the left shoulder is brought forward. The left hand is cupped in front of the face and the left elbow is resting on the back of the right hand. As the step forward is made on the right foot, the right shoulder is brought forward. The right hand is cupped in front of the face and the right elbow is resting on the back of the left hand.

CHAPTER X
Class Organization

There is no definite pattern of class organization which fits all situations and which can be adequately administered by all individual teachers. Therefore, a social dance teacher must rely a great deal upon his own initiative and ability to put across to the student the material which is believed to be essential. This implies that a teacher will have to sift out the materials and the ways of presenting these materials which best fit the situation. For example, if a teacher has allotted just a short time to teach social dancing, only a few of the rhythms and perhaps the basic steps in each of these rhythms would be all that a teacher could get across. If the teacher has been allotted a great deal of time to teach social dancing, many rhythms, along with their basic steps and several variations in each of the rhythms could be covered.

Each teacher will also have to determine the manner in which social dancing will be taught. For example, if dancing has to be taught in a small area, class organization will have to be fitted to the space allotted.

In order to assist the teacher in putting on a dance program, the following suggestions may prove helpful:

1. In order to have a socially homogeneous group, an effort should be made to have all students know each other. Each student should have a name tag which he wears until everyone is known by name.

2. During the class period, continual changing of partners should be made. This gives the opportunity to socialize with all, as well as the opportunity to dance with many different partners.

3. It is important to stress to the class that a good dancer is one who knows the steps. It is, therefore, very important that the individuals know the step before having them dance with partners.

4. In teaching a person to dance, it becomes very important that a certain amount of time be spent in rhythm training. Perhaps the easiest way to accomplish this is to set up situations in which the entire group moves about as a unit in time with the music. As this group moves about, the teacher can pick out those individuals who are having trouble sensing the rhythm and give them special attention. It also affords those individuals who are having difficulty sensing the rhythm to feel the unity of the group and to get in step with the entire group.

A rhythm band situation could be set up to teach the various rhythms. The simplest way is to have the gentlemen clap the pattern and the ladies the accent. For variation, this could then be repeated by having the gentlemen clap the accent and the ladies the pattern. For example, in the waltz, which is three-quarter time, there are three quarter notes to a measure of music and each quarter note receives one count. The accent falls on the first count of each measure. Therefore, the gentlemen clap on the count of one, two, and three while the ladies clap on the count of one only. In the variation, the ladies clap on the count of one, two, and three while the gentlemen clap on the count of one only.

5. Since the range of abilities within any class is great, the teacher must at all times attempt to present a simple approach and simple materials in order that all students will learn. Occasionally difficult steps should be presented in order that those who have picked up the simple steps will be challenged.

6. During instructional time it is a good idea to review materials that were given in a previous class period, present new materials, allow time for class drills, and give opportunity for practice. During the free practice the instructor should try to assist those individuals who are not progressing as rapidly as they should.

7. One of the ways in which students may be assisted in maintaining the correct social dance position is to have them raise their elbows to the side during all practice periods. When the dancers realize that they must hold their own arms up, it will make them aware of the fact that they must not lean on their partner for support when dancing.

8. Perhaps the best way to have the class organized to teach a step is to have the ladies in a line facing the center of the floor and the gentlemen across from them and facing them. The instructor can then take his or her place between the lines, alternately facing the groups and doing the step in the correct direction. This gives the instructor an opportunity to watch half the class at a time to see if they are moving correctly.

OOOOOOOOOOOOOOOO

I

XXXXXXXXXXXXXX

An alternate way to use this same formation is to have both lines facing the same direction, with the instructor out in front. Many instructors like to teach the gentlemen's part to the ladies. If this is desirable, the instructor can then have both lines facing the same direction and place himself in front of them, having both groups moving in the same direction.

I

O O O O O O O O O O O O O O O O

X X X X X X X X X X X X X X X X

O O O O O O O   In the use of these formations, the instructor should be very careful to realize that he may place himself in a position that his back may be to part of the group. Therefore, the instructor should continually
X X X X X X X   change his direction in order to observe all students and to be seen by them.

9. From the formations illustrated in #8, the gentlemen could move forward to the ladies' line to pick up partners. If this line is too long, it is very easy to have every other couple move back forming another line of couples in order to practice the dance.

O O O O O O O   10. Another favorite formation for teaching social dance is to have a large circle with an alternation of ladies and gentlemen. In this formation it is a good idea to have the circle move forward, which is
X X X X X X X   always counterclockwise in social dance.

This formation may also be used by having the ladies face their partners. This type of formation is of particular value in getting the couples to move in time with the music. In this way those who are having trouble maintaining the correct rhythm may be picked out.

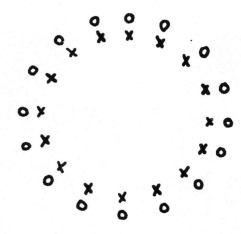

11. Another circle formation which can be used is one in which the gentlemen form a circle inside that of the ladies, facing away from the center of the circle, while the ladies face the center of the circle. This formation is very useful in teaching the various step patterns in which the couples progress in a sideward direction.

12. In order to get the individuals to move together, the instructor will find it helpful to use the commands "ready" - "and".

MUSIC FOR SOCIAL DANCE

Musical accompaniment for teaching social dance usually consists of a piano or an electrical record player. If a variety of rhythms are to be taught, the electrical record player is the more desirable.

The record player should be adequate for the size of the dance room and for the size of the group. It should have a speed control so that the tempo of the music can be adjusted, a lever adjustment to provide for the various types of records on the market, and an adjustment to control the pitch and the volume. In many situations it may be necessary for the instructor to use a microphone. Therefore a record player should have a microphone which can be used. The record player, because of its many adjustments, should be inspected regularly to minimize electrical or mechanical failures.

A set of rules governing the use of the record player should be established. For example, it may be desired that only the instructor should handle the operation of the record player rather than let all students handle it. Perhaps some member or members of the class might be trained in the use of the record player.

The ideal record player is a "juke box" holding a large number of records sufficient to have a large selection in all the rhythms used in social dance. With the "juke box", all that is necessary is to push a button to play the desired records.

RECORDS

A choice of records is usually an individual preference since most teachers have their favorites for teaching. The choice of records changes from time to time depending upon current "hits" and old favorites. Various age groups like certain types of music. With the assistance of the group, records should be obtained which are popular for that particular group. Particularly for beginners, records with vocals and records with breaks in which the rhythm is not pronounced should be avoided. Records that have a consistent rhythm throughout the record and in which the rhythm is definitely pronounced are the most desirable for beginners.

CHAPTER XI
Organization and Promotion of a Dance

A dance is one of the social functions which is attractive to individuals of all ages. It is a medium through which youth of opposite sexes meet each other in a desirable atmosphere. Not only does a dance serve young people, but people of all ages enjoy this social activity. However, in order that all individuals at a dance may enjoy it to the fullest extent, there should be a working organization behind the scenes so that the affair will progress in a smooth fashion.

The organizational arrangement for a dance depends a great deal upon the local situation and the size and type of dance. The organization presented here may serve as a model for those faced with the problem of putting on a dance. The first large committee is a central committee supervised by a general chairman whose duty it is to appoint sub-committees and to supervise the work of these sub-committees. There should be close working arrangements between the central committee and each of the sub-committees, with frequent reports of progress of the sub-committee to the central committee by way of the general chairman. In some organizations this central committee is made up of the chairman of each of the sub-committees.

The following sub-committees are suggested:

1. <u>Publicity Committee</u>:

a. The publicity committee is charged with the responsibility of advertising the dance so that it will be a success as far as attendance is concerned.

b. If the dance is an invitational one, this committee should assume the responsibility of sending out invitations and giving proper publicity to encourage those who receive the invitations to attend.

c. Such methods as using posters, leaflets, newspapers, personal contacts, telephone, invitations, and radio are some of the means this committee could use.

d. It is responsible for the removal of all materials used by the committee in publicizing the dance.

2. <u>Program Committee</u>:

a. The program committee is charged with the responsibility of making the dance enjoyable for all those who attend.

b. It is concerned with obtaining a proper place in which to hold the dance.

c. It should be responsible for the selection of the orchestra. If an electrical pick-up or a "juke box" is used, this committee is responsible to see that it is available and in working order.

d. It should be concerned with the choice of music.

e. If entertainment is wanted, this committee should obtain the performers.

f. It is responsible for the return of any props which were obtained for the entertainers or any materials which were obtained for the musicians. If an electrical pick-up was used, it should see that it is returned to its proper place, along with any records.

3. <u>Business Committee</u>:

a. This committee is charged with the responsibility of all financial matters of the dance. This includes all disbursements and receipts.

b. It should contract for the printing. This involves tickets, programs, and all other printed materials.

c. Ticket takers should be a responsibility of this committee.

4. <u>Wardrobe Committee</u>:

a. This committee is charged with the responsibility of the rest rooms and the handling of the checking service.

b. It should work out a suitable checking system and see to it that it is properly handled

c. It should appoint a matron for the ladies' rest room and an attendant for the men's room.

5. <u>Refreshment Committee</u>:

a. This committee is charged with the responsibility of providing the foods and drinks for the dance.

b. It should determine the type of refreshments desired.

c. It should also consider very carefully where the refreshments will be served.

d. It should provide adequate facilities for the disposal of any waste items such as paper cups and dishes, or other items.

e. It should appoint someone to see to it that the rules governing the consumption of the refreshments are carried out.

f. This committee should also be responsible for the decorations needed for the refreshment table.

6. Decoration Committee:

a. The decoration committee is charged with the responsibility of converting the place in which the dance is to be held into a desirable setting.

b. It should determine the nature of the decorations.

c. It should purchase the supplies needed for decorating.

d. It should be responsible for removing all decorations that are used as soon as possible after the dance is over.

7. Hostess Committee:

a. The hostess committee is charged with the responsibility of inviting chaperons and special guests to the dance.

b. It should be responsible for welcoming and introducing all guests.

c. If there is to be a receiving line, it should assume the responsibility of organizing it.

CHAPTER XII
Mixers

At a dance it is desirable to encourage the participants to exchange partners. Many individuals exchange partners very readily with their friends. However, there is a tendency ⌐ to exchange with individuals who are not so well known. Social dance mixers are devices or methods that are used to get a dance under way, to give variety to the dance, to help break up the evening, or to encourage the exchange of partners.

GRAND MARCH

The music used for the grand march is usually a series of slow marches. The ladies form a line on one side of the room and the gentlemen line up on the other side of the room so that when the lines move to the rear of the room and come together, meeting in the center, the lady will be on the gentleman's right. When they meet, the lady takes the gentleman's right arm and they march down the center together toward the bandstand, followed by all others in the line so that they are paired off. As soon as all have partners, the leader may call, "All dance", or he may continue to lead them in another grand march variation, some of which are as follows:

1. First couple to the right and second couple to the left. They continue to circle around the outside of the dance floor.

2. When the couples come toward each other in the rear, the leader calls, "Down the center by fours".

3. When the first four reach the front, the leader calls, "First four to the right, second four to the left".

4. These fours continue around the outside of the dance floor and when they meet in the rear, the leader calls out, "Down the center by eights".

5. When these eight reach the front, the leader calls, "Four to the right and four to the left". These groups continue around the outside of the dance floor.

6. When these fours meet in the center, the leader calls, "Down the center by fours". When this call comes, first one side turns down the center then the other side turns behind them.

7. When these fours reach the front of the dance floor, the leader then calls, "Two to the right and two to the left".

8. The couples continue around the dance floor until they meet in the rear. When they meet, the leader calls, "Down the center by twos". When this call comes, first one side turns down the center then the other side turns behind them.

9. When the first couple reaches the front of the room, the leader calls, "All dance".

ARCH

The ladies form a line on one side of the room and the gentlemen form a line on the other side. These lines march across the back of the room and meet each other. As the lady and gentleman meet, they join hands and raise their arms to form an arch. The next lady and gentleman meet, join hands and go under the arch. This couple, after going under the arch, immediately forms another arch. Each lady and gentleman continues in turn to meet in the center, go under the arch, and then immediately form a similar arch next to the last couple under whose raised arms they passed. When all couples have formed a total arch, the head or lead couple comes under all the raised arms, followed in turn by the second, third, and all other couples. This continues until the leader calls, "All dance".

CIRCLE MIXER

Ladies join hands and form a circle in the center of the floor. The gentlemen join hands and form a circle around the outside of the ladies circle. The gentlemen move to the right and the ladies to the left. When the music stops, the ladies turn around and face the outside circle and each man dances with the lady in front of him.

A variation of this would be to have the ladies join hands and form a circle facing away from the center of the circle.

If there are more gentlemen than ladies, or more ladies then gentlemen, they could be allowed to "cut in" when the dance starts.

GRAND RIGHT AND LEFT

A large circle is made by the gentleman placing the lady on his right and all couples joining hands. The hands are dropped and partners face each other and join right hands. The gentlemen move forward counter-clockwise, the ladies move forward clockwise, passing right shoulder to right shoulder. Each gives his left hand to the next dancer and passes left shoulder to left shoulder. This continues, alternating right and left hands, until the music stops. Then each gentleman dances with the lady he is then facing.

If the leader desires to continue this mixer, he will call for a large circle with the grand right and left repeated until the music stops. Then the gentleman dances with the lady he is facing.

COUPLES CHANGE

This is started by having all the couples on the floor dancing. The leader calls, "Change partners with nearest couple". This may be done several times during the dance.

A variation of this is to inform the group that they are to change partners with the next couple when the music stops. The music could be stopped several times during one dance.

SHOE MIXER

Have all the ladies meet in the center of the floor. Request that they take off their left shoe and place it in a pile in the middle of the floor and then hop to the outside of the room. When the music starts, the gentlemen go to the center and select a shoe. They must then find the owner and dance with her.

DOUBLING DANCERS

Select a small number of couples to start dancing in the middle of the floor while all other couples are around the outside of the floor. When the music stops the gentlemen go to the outside and select a lady to dance. At the same time the ladies go to the outside and select a gentleman to dance. This continues with several starts and stops of the music until all are dancing.

EXPLANATION OF SYMBOLS USED IN DIAGRAMS

I - Instructor

L - Left foot

O - Lady

P - Pulse or accent which has an increased emphasis.

Q - Quick. A quick step is done to one beat of music, and two
     quick steps equal one slow step.

R - Right foot

S - Slow. A slow step is done to two beats of music, and it
    takes the same amount of time as two quick steps.

X - Gentleman

𝄽 - Quarter rest

♪ - Staccato; - Note is cut short in playing.

BIBLIOGRAPHY

Ballwebber, Edith. Group Instruction in Social Dancing. New York: A.S. Barnes and Company, 1938. 131 pp.

Butler, Albert. "The New Trend in Social Dance Instruction". Journal of Health and Physical Education, IX:6, June, 1938. p. 362.

Byrnes, Don and Alice Swanson. "Mambo". Dance Magazine, XXV:10, October, 1951. pp. 29, 36, 38.

Dean, Virginia. "Social Dancing for Fifth and Sixth Grades". Journal of Health and Physical Education, IX:4, April, 1938. p. 220.

Duggan, Anne S. "The Place of Dance in the School Physical Education Program". Journal of Health and Physical Education, XXII:3, March, 1951. p. 26.

Duran, Gustavo. Recordings of Latin American Songs and Dances. Washington, D.C.: Division of Music and Visual Arts, Department of Cultural Affairs, Pan American Union, 1950. 92 pp.

Faust, George I. "A Workable Method for Teaching Social Dancing". Journal of Health and Physical Education, XI:1, January, 1940. p. 42.

Glass, Henry. "Social Dancing for Junior High Schools". Journal of Health and Physical Education, XVI:3, March, 1945. p. 130.

Hinkel, Delta T. "Coeducational Social Dance". Journal of Health and Physical Education, XI:5, May, 1940. p. 298.

Hinman, Mary Wood. "Educational Possibilities of the Dance". Journal of Health and Physical Education, V:4, April, 1934. p. 4.

Hostetler, Lawrence. The Art of Social Dancing. New York: A. S. Barnes and Company, 1930. 169 pp.

Hostetler, Lawrence. "Social Dancing, From Schoolroom to Ballroom". Journal of Health and Physical Education, X:2, February, 1939. p. 76.

Hussey, Delia P. "Children Consider the Dance Program". Journal of Health and Physical Education, XVI:1, January, 1945. p. 34.

Marsh, Agnes. "Social Dancing as a Project in Physical Education". Journal of Health and Physical Education, IV:2, February, 1933. p. 28

Moore, J. "An Examination in Social Dance". Journal of Health and Physical Education, XIX:7, September, 1948. p. 498.

Murray, Arthur. "How To Dance the Mambo". Compact. May, 1953. pp. 80-81.

Parson, Thomas. Popular Ballroom Dances For All. New York: Barnes and Noble, Inc., 1947. 73 pp.

Riggs, John and Francis P. Moussear. "Social Dancing in the Junior College Curriculum". Journal of Health and Physical Education, XXI:1, January, 1950. p. 9.

Russell, Naomi. "Social Dancing". Journal of Health and Physical Education, X:2, February, 1939. p. 88.

Slonimsky, Nicola. <u>Music of Latin America</u>. New York: Thomas Y. Crowell Company, 1945. 374 pp.

Waglow, I. F. "An Experiment in Social Dance Testing". <u>The Research Quarterly</u>, XXIV:1, March, 1953. pp. 97-101.

Waglow, I. F. "Jitterbug, A Teaching Progression". <u>The Physical Educator</u>, IX:4, December, 1952. pp. 119-121.

Index

CPSIA information can be obtained
at www.ICGtesting.com
Printed in the USA
BVOW07s1440200417
481729BV00018B/75/P